French - Spanish

LEARNING FLASHCARDS

FOR BABIES TODDLERS

alligator

caimán

The alligator is having a party.

fourmi

hormiga

The ant is red.

ours

oso

The bear loves you.

abeille

abeja

The bee is saying hello.

oiseau

pájaro

The bird is flying.

papillon

mariposa

The butterfly is pretty.

chameau

camello

The camel has a hump.

chat

gato

The cat is happy.

dinosaure

dinosaurio

The dinosaur is laying eggs.

poulet

pollo

The chicken is dancing.

vache

vaca

The cow has a bell.

cerf

ciervo

The reindeer has a toy.

chien

perro

The dog has two floppy ears.

dauphin

delfín

The dolphin is swimming.

canard

pato

The duck has a bow.

aigle

águila

The eagle is looking for food.

l'éléphant

elefante

The elephant is sitting.

poisson

pez

The fish is a clownfish.

libellule

libélula

The dragonfly is blue.

renard

zorro

The fox has a red nose.

grenouille

rana

The frog is smiling.

girafe

jirafa

The giraffe has a long neck.

chèvre

cabra

The goat has a beard

ver de terre

gusano

The worm is in the apple

poule

gallina

The hen has chicks.

hippopotame

hipopótamo

The hippo is big.

cheval

caballo

The horse is fast.

kangourou

canguro

The kangaroo has a baby.

chaton

gatito

The kitten is playing.

lion

león

The lion has a mane.

homard

langosta

The lobster is red.

singe

mono

The monkey has a tail.

poulpe

pulpo

The octopus has food.

hibou

búho

The owls have big eyes.

panda

panda

The panda wears a diaper.

porc

cerdo

The pig is fat and pink.

chiot

perrito

The dog is brown.

lapin

conejo

The rabbit has a carrot.

rat

rata

The mouse is writing something.

crabe

cangrejo

The crab has two pinchers.

requin

tiburón

The shark is scary.

mouton

oveja

The sheep are very fluffy.

escargot

caracol

The snail is slow.

serpent

serpiente

The snake has poison.

araignée

araña

The spider is purple.

écureuil

ardilla

The squirrel has a nut.

tigre

tigre

The tiger has a red bow.

tortue

tortuga

The turtle has a shell.

loup

lobo

The wolf is smiling.

zèbre

cebra

The zebra is black and white.

dinde

pavo

The turkey has two legs.

coq

gallo

The rooster will crow.

perroquet

loro

The parrot is colorful.

hérisson

erizo

The hedgehog has apples.

pomme

manzana

The apple has a leaf.

abricot

albaricoque

The apricot is yellow.

avocat

aguacate

The avocado has a nut.

banane

plátano

The banana is yellow.

la mûre

mora

There are a lot of blackberries.

cassis

grosella negra

The blackcurrants are yummy.

myrtille

arándano

The blueberries are sweet.

cerise

cereza

The cherries have a stem.

noix de coco

coco

The coconuts have juice.

figues

higos

The fig has seeds.

grain de raisin

uva

The grapes are purple.

pamplemousse

pomelo

The grapefruits are sour.

kiwi

kiwi

The kiwi is fresh.

citron

limón

The lemons are yellow.

citron vert

lima

We have lots of lime.

litchi

lychee

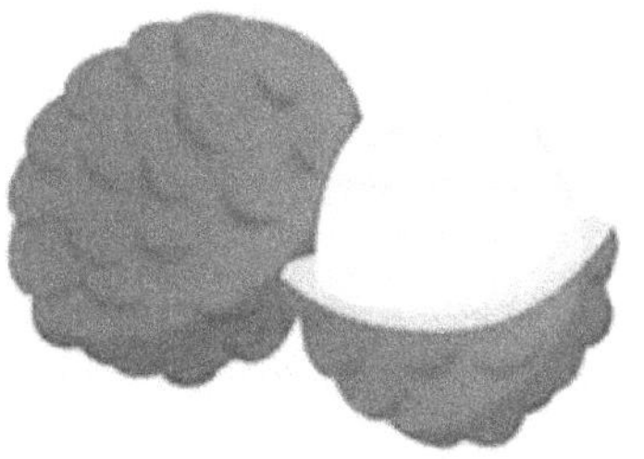

I like to eat lychee.

mandarine

mandarina

Oranges are refreshing.

mangue

mango

Mango is my favorite fruit.

orange

naranja

Mandarins are like oranges.

papaye

papaya

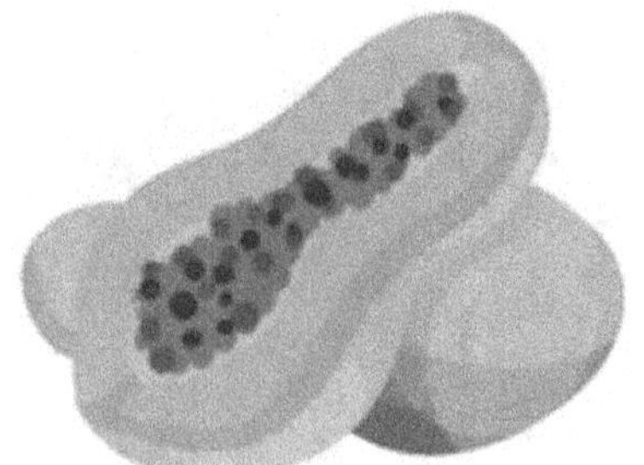

Papayas have lots of seeds.

pêche

melocotón

Peaches are juicy.

poire

pera

Pears have a strange figure.

ananas

piña

The pineapple has a thumbs up.

prune

ciruela

Plums are healthy for you.

grenade

granada

Pomegranates are all red.

framboise

frambuesa

The raspberry is shiny.

fraise

fresa

The strawberry has leaves on top.

pastèque

sandía

The watermelon is big.

mandarine

mandarina

The tangerine looks like an orange.

tarte

tarta

I like to eat apple pie.

gâteau

pastel

That cake is huge.

bonbons

caramelo

Candy is not good for your teeth.

biscuit

galleta

Cookies are easy to make.

donut

rosquilla

I like strawberry donuts.

crème glacée

helado

The ice cream is melting.

muffin

mollete

The muffin has a cute wrapper.

pudding

pudín

We eat pudding on Christmas.

classeur

aglutinante

I keep pictures in my binder.

livre

libro

I like to eat books.

sac à dos

mochila

The backpack has lots of stuff.

les ciseaux

tijeras

I have scissors in my bag.

épingles

patas

Pins can hold stuff up.

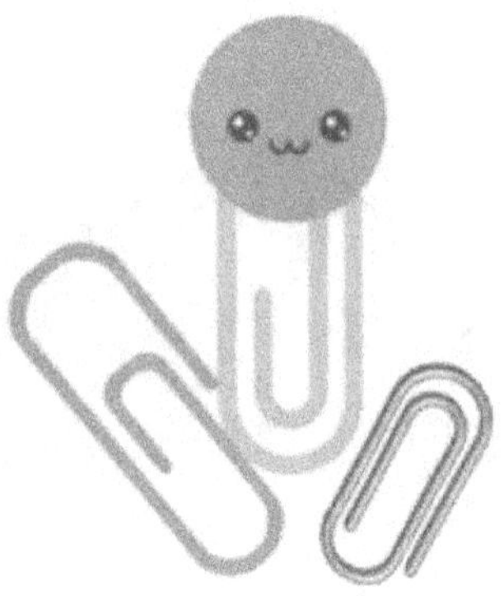

Clips can hold up paper.

I have lots of paper.

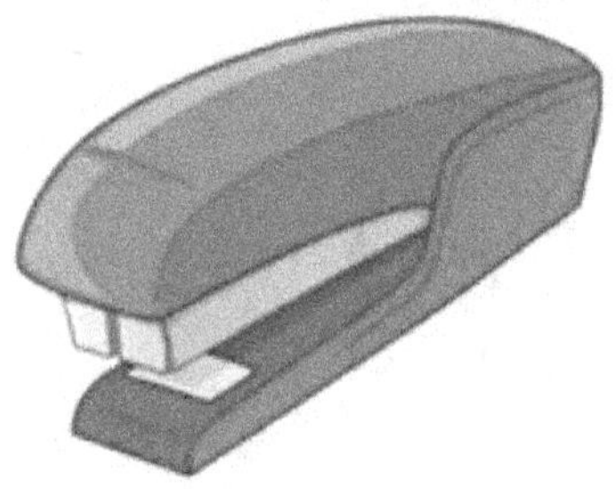

My stapler is shiny and red.

My calculator has buttons.

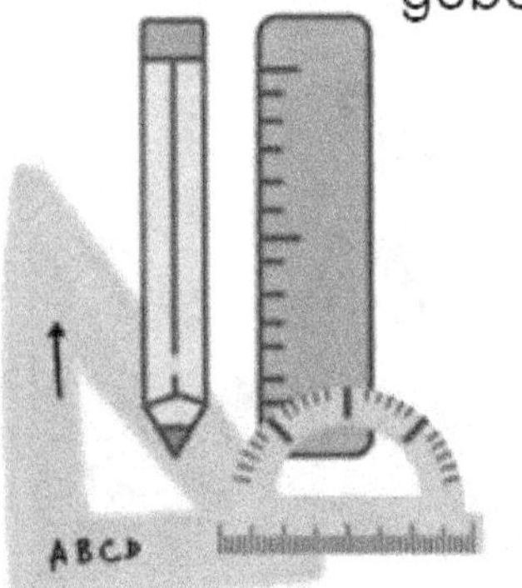

I have lots of rulers.

The glue is sticky.

bibliothèque

librero

My bookcase has lots of things.

calendrier

calendario

I have a calendar on my table.

chaise

silla

My chair is fancy.

l'horloge

reloj

The clock says that it's 3 o'clock.

ordinateur

computadora

I do things on my computer.

bureaux

escritorios

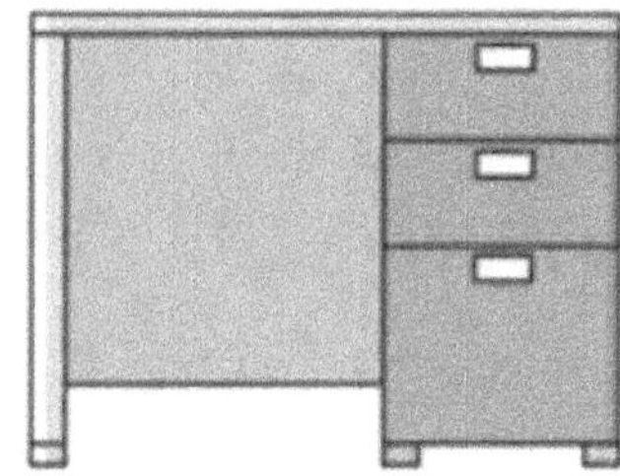

I put lots of things on my desk.

dictionnaire

diccionario

The dictionary has lots of words.

la gomme

borrador

Erasers are used with pencils.

carte

mapa

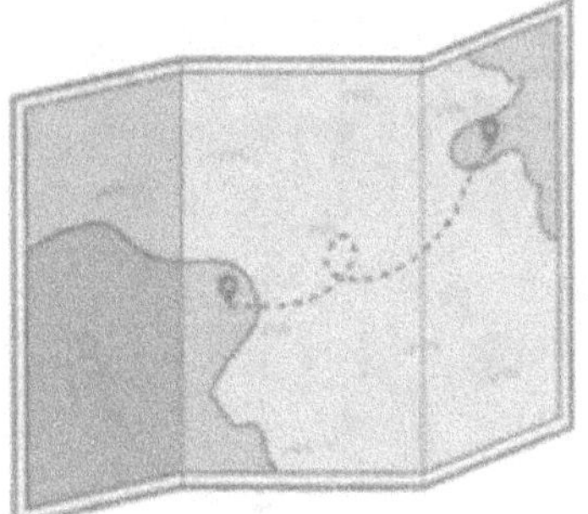

The map shows you different places.

carnet

cuaderno

I use notebooks at school.

stylo

bolígrafo

My pen is very pretty.

crayon

lápiz

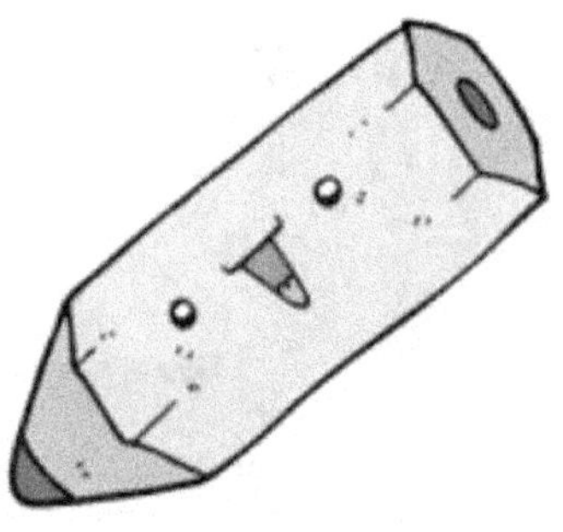

My friend gave me a pencil.

ceinture

cinturón

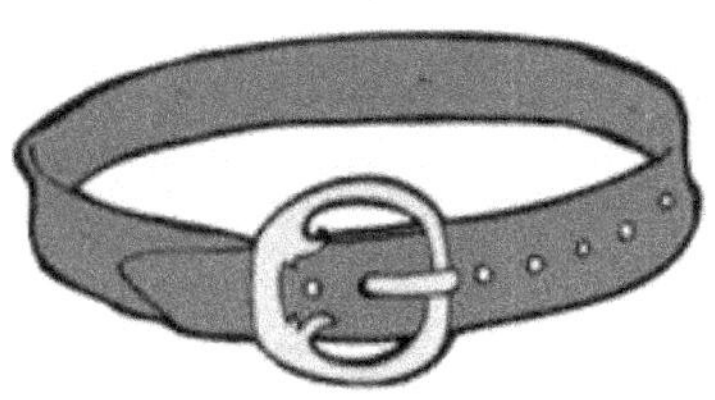

I have a belt on my pants.

bottes

botas

I have big brown boots.

chapeau

sombrero

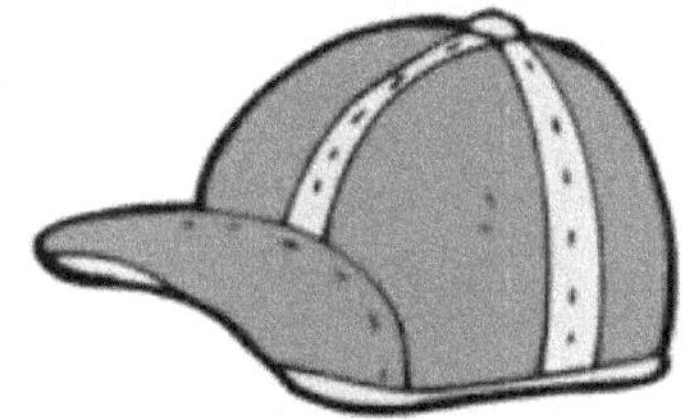

My mom bought me a new cap.

manteau

saco

She has a long yellow coat.

robes

vestidos

My dress has a bow.

gants

guantes

I got new gloves.

chapeau

sombrero

That hat is for a wicked witch.

veste

chaqueta

The jacket is cozy.

jeans

pantalones

My jeans are long.

pyjamas

pijama

I sleep in my pajamas.

un pantalon

pantalones

The bear is wearing pants.

imperméable

impermeable

We wear our raincoats when it is raining.

écharpe

bufanda

The baby has a scarf around his neck.

chemise

camisa

I like this shirt the best.

des chaussures

zapatos

I have red and blue shoes.

jupe

falda

My skirt has lots of buttons.

pantalon

pantalones

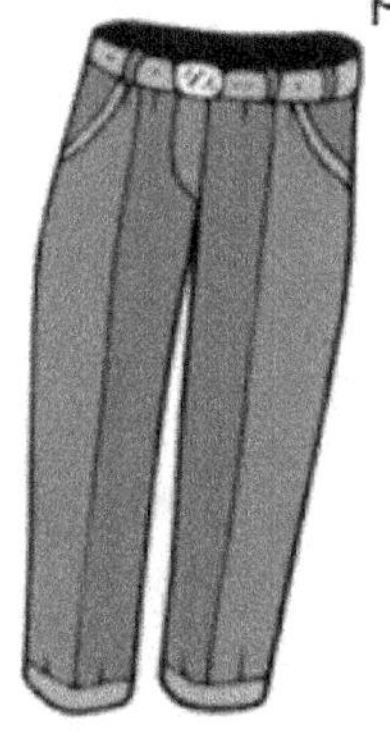

My dad wears slacks.

chaussons

zapatillas

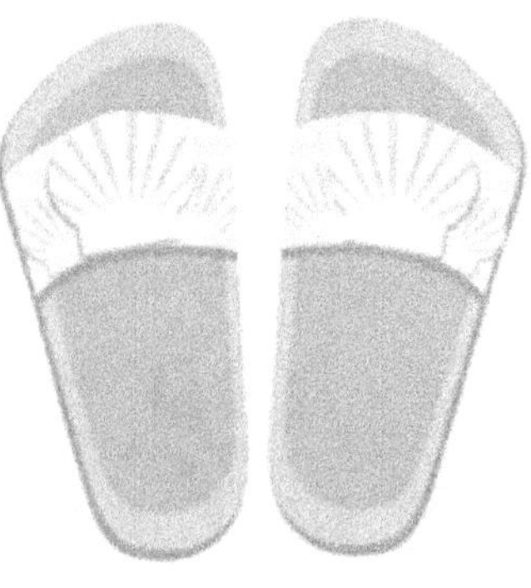

I have seashells on my sandals.

chaussettes

calcetines

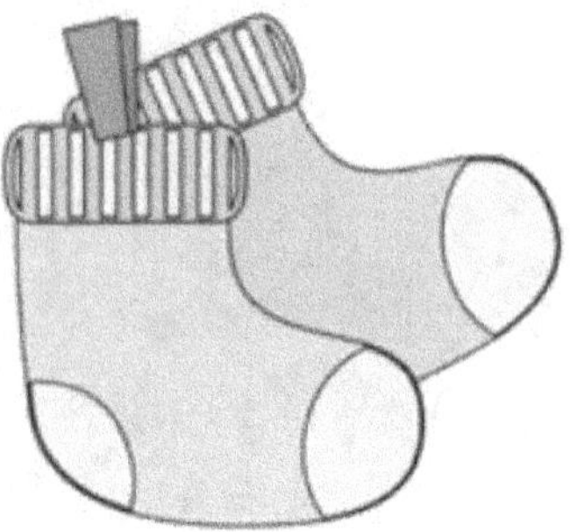

My baby sister wears socks.

costume

traje

My brother is wearing a suit.

chandail

suéter

I am wearing a sweater for winter.

cravate

corbata

My dad wears a tie to meetings.

pantalon

pantalones

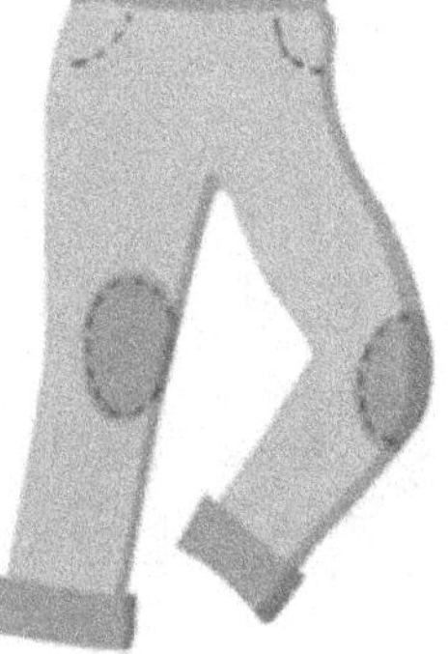

The trousers look like jeans.

slip

calzoncillos

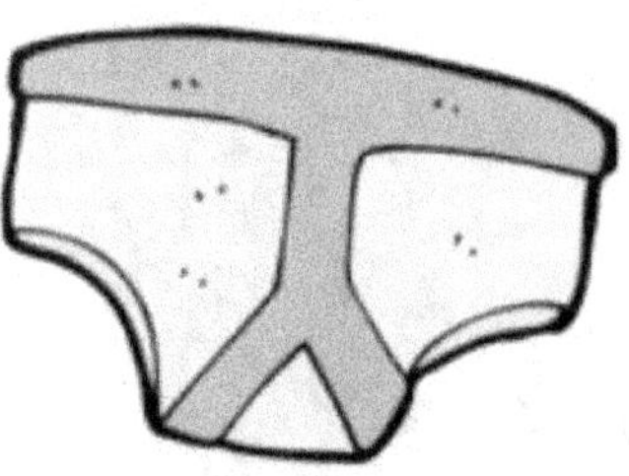

I always wear my underwear.

maillot de corps

camiseta

My undershirt has a star.

une

uno

Number one and the bee are friends.

deux

dos

The cat and the mouse both love two.

trois

tres

The bear gives number three a present.

quatre

cuatro

Number four is a home for the cat.

cinq

cinco

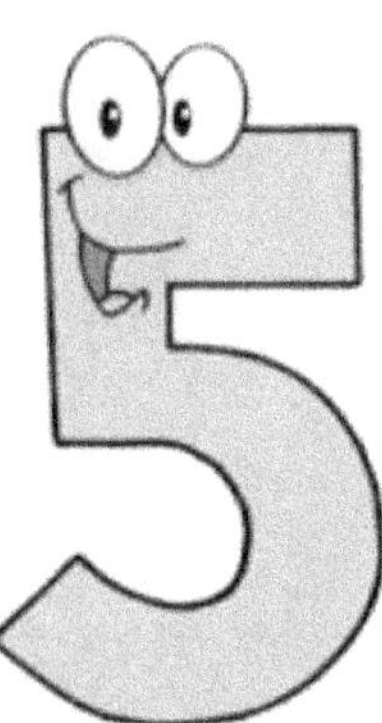

Number five hatches an egg.

six

seis

Number six is going to eat a carrot.

sept

siete

Number seven is playing with the tiger.

huit

ocho

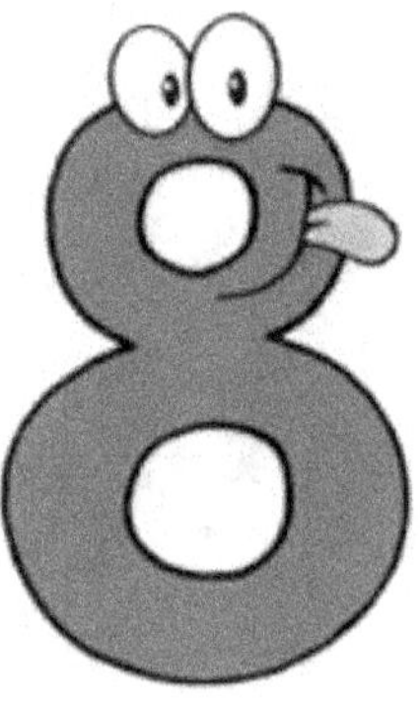

Number eight is funny.

neuf

nueve

Number nine meets the parrot.

dix

diez

Number ten is smiling.

onze

once

Number eleven has big eyes.

douze

doce

Number twelve is number one and two.

treize

trece

Number thirteen is excited.

quatorze

catorce

The number fourteen is vast.

quinze

quince

The number fifteen is green.

seize

dieciséis

Sixteen is my lucky number.

dix-sept

de diecisiete

Number seventeen look alike.

dix-huit

dieciocho

Number eighteen will go to the circus.

dix-neuf

diecinueve

I am nineteen now!

vingt

veinte

Number twenty has a zero.

fourmi

hormiga

The ant has lots of legs.

cloche

campana

The bell will ring.

vache

vaca

The cow has a bow.

poupée

muñeca

She has a cute bear doll.

oeuf

huevo

The chick has hatched out of the egg.

poisson

pez

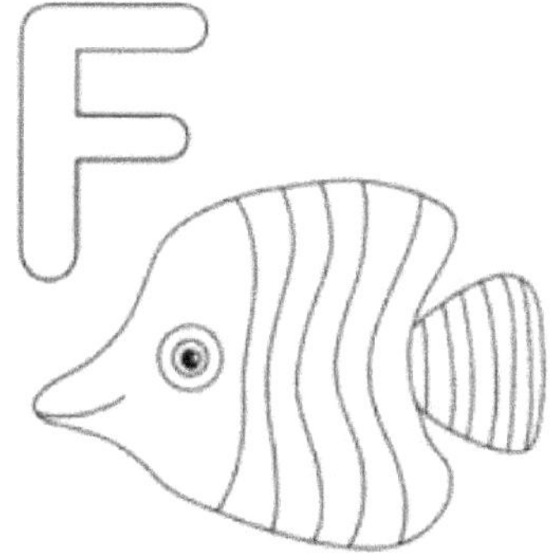

The fish is swimming in the water.

chèvre

cabra

The goat is sitting on the grass.

chapeau

sombrero

He is wearing a hat.

crème glacée

helado

I like to eat ice cream.

confiture

mermelada

The kitten is sitting on the jam jar.

chaton

gatito

The cat is sleeping on the floor.

lion

león

The lion is waiting for the tiger.

rat

rata

The mouse has lots of presents.

nez

nariz

The reindeer has a red nose.

hibou

búho

The owl is sleeping.

porc

cerdo

The pig will eat cupcakes.

reine

reina

The queen has a big crown.

lapin

conejo

The rabbit is jumping up and down.

mouton

oveja

The sheep have fluffy wool.

tortue

tortuga

The turtle has a shell.

parapluie

paraguas

The mouse is holding an umbrella.

van

camioneta

The van is driving along the road.

pastèque

sandía

The watermelon has lots of seeds.

xylophone

xilófono

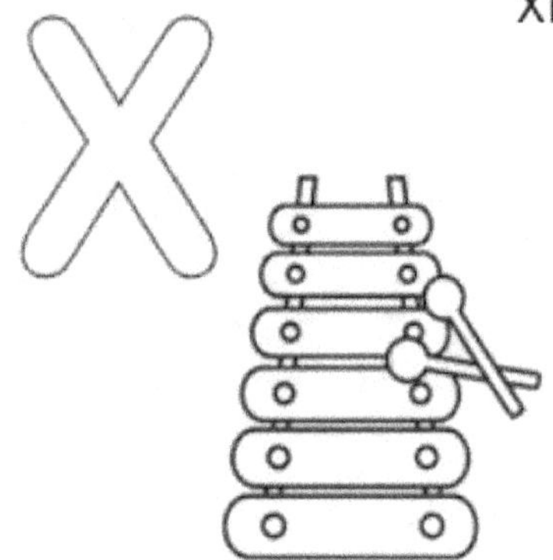

We are going to play the xylophone.

yaourt

yogur

We opened the yogurt can.

zèbre

cebra

The zebra is surprised.

rose

rosado

color the word and
the picture in pink

Most of my clothes are pink.

marron

marrón

color the word and
the picture in pink

brown

My chocolate is brown.

gris

gris

color the word and
the picture in pink

gray

I don't like the color gray.

vert

verde

color the word and
the picture in pink

green

The vegetables are green.

jaune

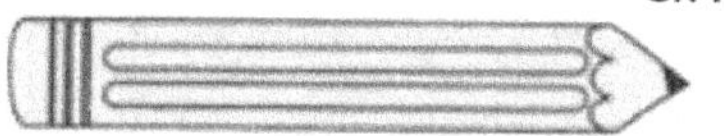

amarillo

color the word and
the picture in pink

yellow

Bananas are yellow.

blanc

blanco

color the word and
the picture in pink

white

The paper that I write on is white.

rouge

rojo

color the word and
the picture in pink

red

Apples are red.

bleu

azul

color the word and
the picture in pink

The night sky is blue.

percer

perforar

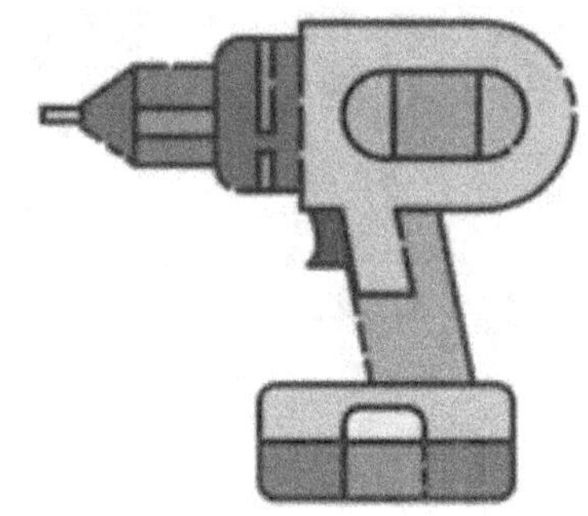

The drill will help us fix this.

marteau

martillo

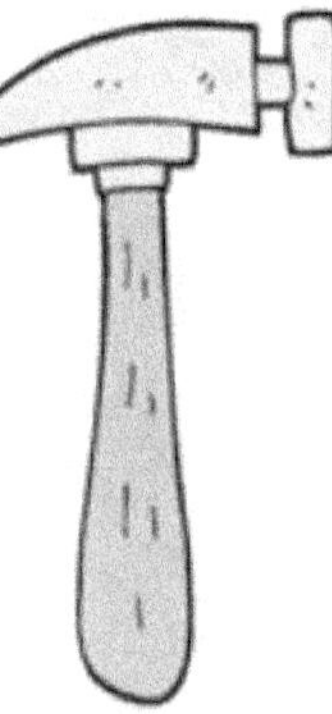

The hammer is going to nail the picture.

couteau

cuchillo

The knife is sharp.

pinces

alicates

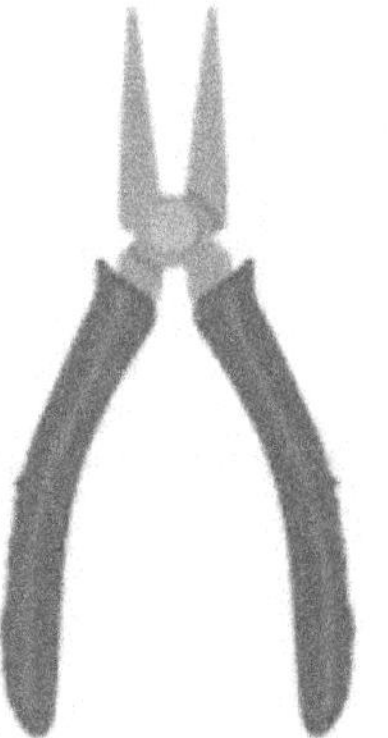

The plier is used for many things.

vu

sierra

The saw can chop wood.

les ciseaux

tijeras

I use scissors to cut paper.

tournevis

destornillador

The screwdriver can screw in the knots.

clé

llave inglesa

The wrench can help unscrew the knots.

avion

avión

The airplane is going to leave now.

vélo

bicicleta

The bicycle is beautiful.

bateau

barco

The boat is floating on the water.

autobus

autobús

The bus is going to school.

voiture

coche

The car is green.

hélicoptère

helicóptero

The helicopter is looking for something.

cheval

caballo

You can ride the horse.

jet

jet

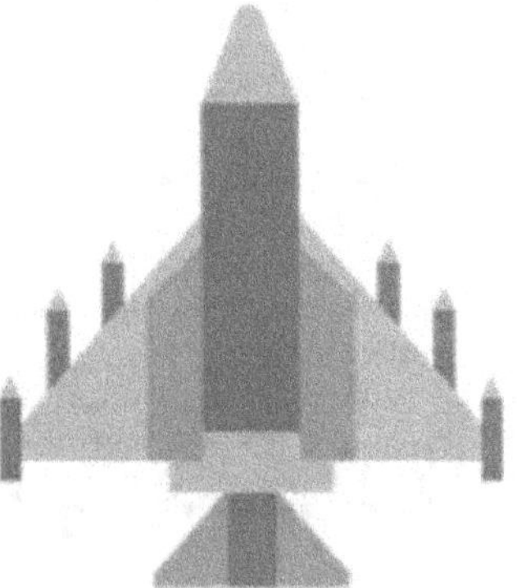

The jet is high-speed.

moto

motocicleta

The motorcycle is on the road.

navire

embarcacion

The ship is on the water.

métro

subterraneo

My mom goes on the subway to work.

taxi

taxi

The taxi has someone inside.

train

entrenar

The train is going slowly.

un camion

camión

The truck has stuff in it.

asperges

espárragos

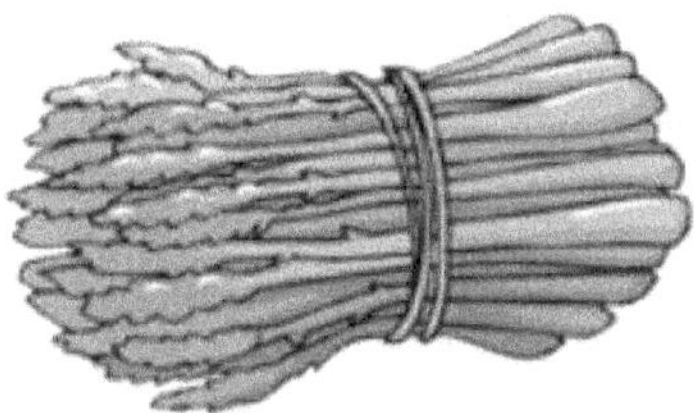

The asparagus is in a bundle.

des haricots

frijoles

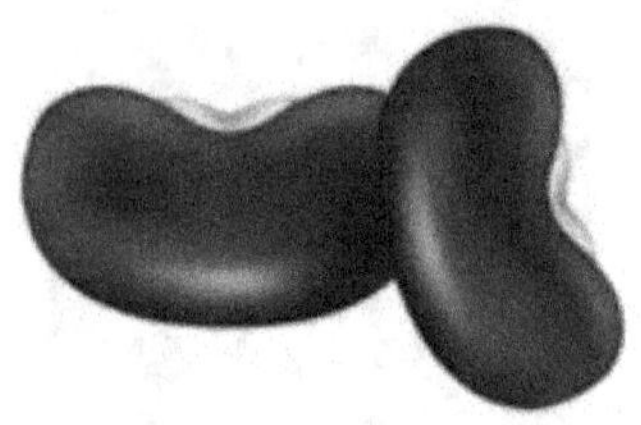

The beans are smooth.

brocoli

brócoli

The broccoli is dancing.

chou

repollo

Bunnies like to eat cabbage.

carotte

zanahoria

The carrots are very long.

céleri

apio

The celery has lots of leaves.

blé

maíz

Corn soup is delicious.

concombre

pepino

The cucumbers are cut into pieces.

aubergine

berenjena

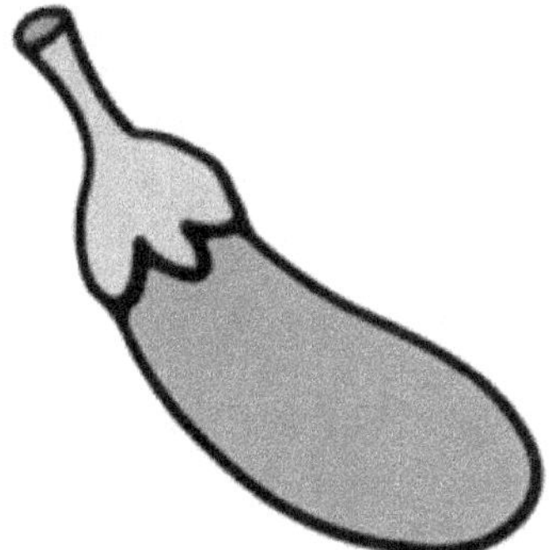

The eggplant is purple.

poivre vert

pimiento verde

The green pepper is juicy.

salade

lechuga

The lettuce is all green.

oignon

cebolla

The onions make my eyes water.

pois

chícharos

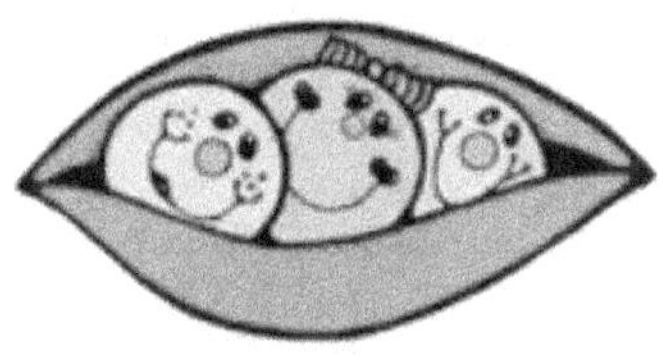

The peas are all in a pod.

patate

patata

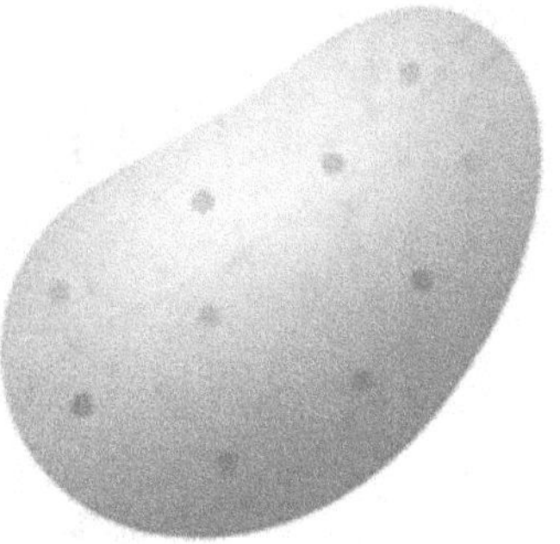

The potato is very shiny.

citrouille

calabaza

The pumpkin is for Halloween.

un radis

rábano

The radish is a type of vegetable.

épinard

espinacas

The spinach is good with cheese.

patate douce

batata

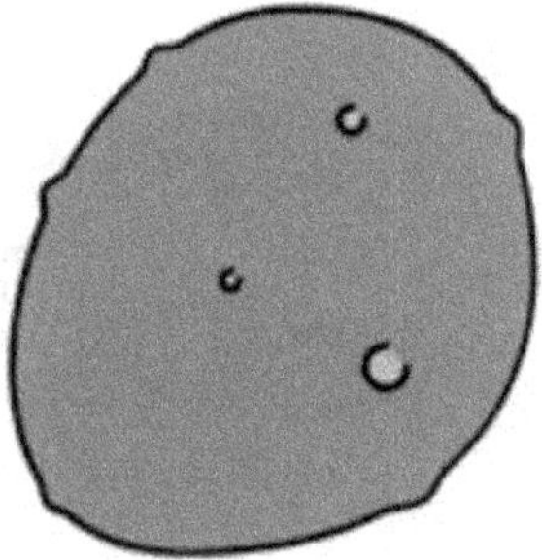

The sweet potato is quite sweet.

tomate

tomate

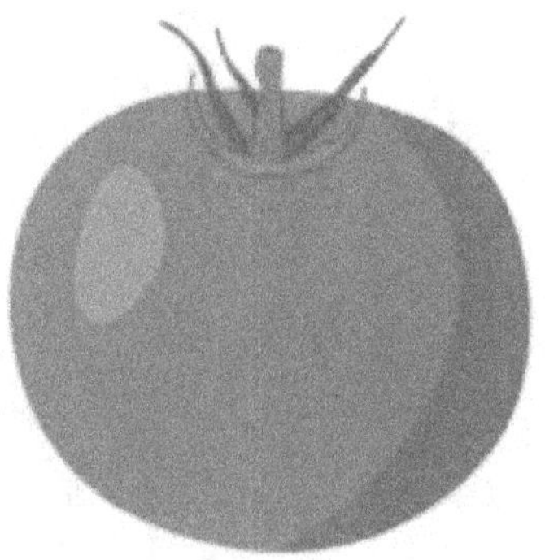

I don't like to eat tomatoes.

navet

nabo

My mom bought some turnips.

nuageux

nublado

The weather is cloudy today.

du froid

frío

I like cold weather.

cool

frio

The temperature is cold today.

brumeux

brumoso

The fog is so strong I can't see the city.

chaud

caliente

The fire is burning hot.

humide

húmedo

It's so humid and wet today.

pluvieux

lluvioso

It's raining very hard.

neigeux

nevado

Welcome to snow land!

orageux

tormentoso

I hate the stormy weather.

ensoleillé

soleado

The sun is shining!

chaud

calentar

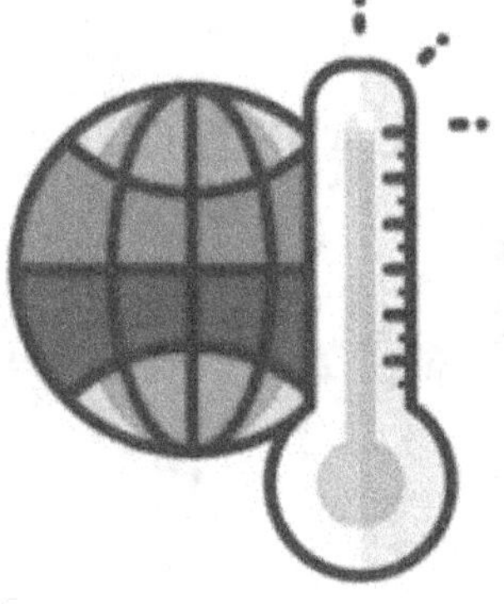

The whole world is warm today!

venteux

ventoso

The leaves are blowing away since it's so windy!

tante

tía

My aunt is very nice to me.

frère

hermano

My brother is very fun to play with.

cousin

prima

I love going to the playground with my cousin.

fille

hija

I like to read books with my daughter.

père

padre

My father is playing with me.

petite fille

nieta

My granddaughter has blond hair.

grand-mère

abuela

My grandmother is very old and has glasses.

petit fils

nieto

My grandson and I are very excited today!

mère

madre

My mother likes to pick me up.

neveu

sobrino

My father's nephew is my cousin.

nièce

sobrina

My niece is very good at playing ball.

sœur

hermana

My sister is so pretty!

fils

hijo

My son likes to play with toy cars.

belle fille

hijastra

My stepdaughter likes the color orange.

belle-mère

madrastra

My stepmother is pretty.

beau-fils

hijastro

This is my stepson, Greg.

oncle

tío

My uncle tells lots of funny jokes.

bol

cuenco

The bowl has nothing inside.

tasse

taza

My mom drinks her coffee out of a cup.

plat

plato

That dish has a bone inside.

fourchette

tenedor

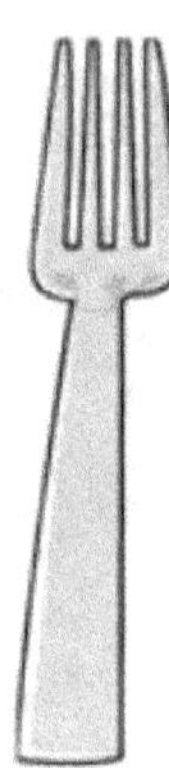

We have more spoons than forks.

verre

vaso

I have a glass of water on my desk.

couteau

cuchillo

I have a knife in my kitchen.

agresser

jarra

This mug of coffee is for my dad.

serviette de table

servilleta

You can use the napkins to clean your hands.

poivre

pimienta

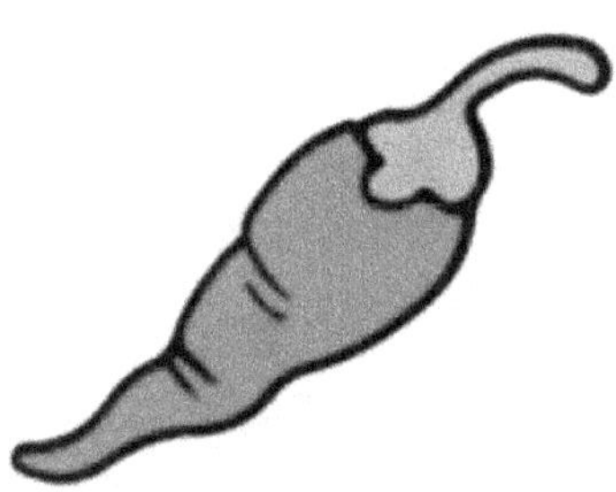

The pepper is very spicy.

lanceur

lanzador

Pour yourself some lemonade from the pitcher.

assiette

plato

Can you help me wash the plates?

salade

ensalada

The salad is very healthy for you.

sel

sal

The salt tastes good with a few pinches of pepper.

soucoupe

platillo

The plate is for my cup.

cuillère

cuchara

I use a spoon to eat my rice.

sucre

azúcar

The pack of sugar is very heavy.

dimanche

domingo

Sunday

Sunday is the day to go to Church!

lundi

lunes

Monday

Monday is the day to start school.

mardi

martes

Tuesday

We will go to the shops on Tuesday.

mercredi

miércoles

Wednesday

Wednesday is hard to spell!

jeudi

jueves

Thursday

Thursday is the fourth day of the week!

vendredi

viernes

Friday

My birthday is on Friday!

samedi

sábado

Saturday

Saturday is the weekend!

cuire

hornear

The chef will bake a cake.

ébullition

hervir

I will boil the eggs.

griller

asar

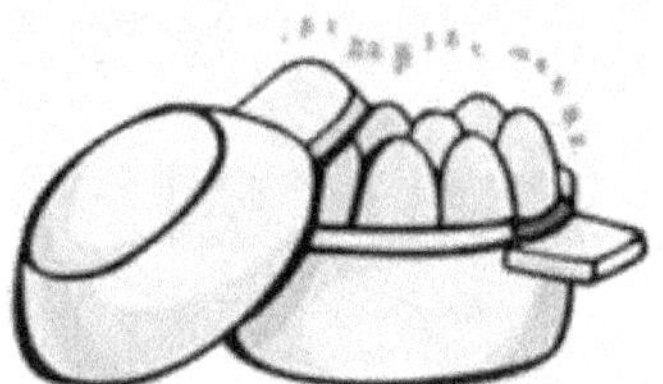

Broil is very yummy.

ouvre-boîte

abrelatas

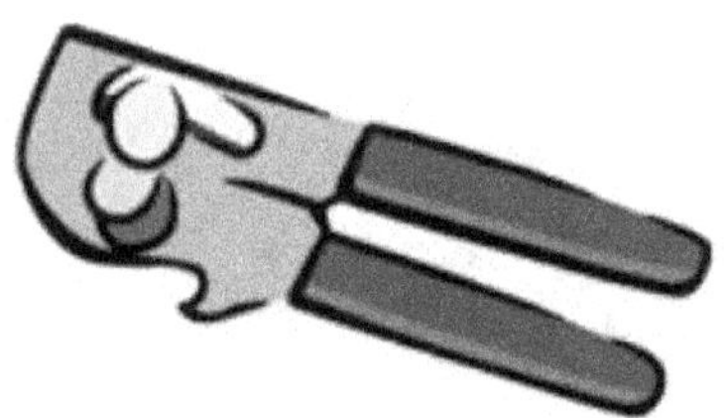

That can opener is used for opening cans.

frire

freír

The pan can fry lots of things.

gril

parrilla

We have a grill in our backyard.

tasse à mesurer

taza medidora

My mom uses the measuring cup for baking.

cuillère à mesurer

cuchara medidora

I use a measuring spoon to eat my dessert.

four micro onde

microonda

The microwave is used to heat food.

bol à mélanger

tazón para mezclar

She is using the mixing bowl to mix things.

serviettes en papier

toallas de papel

Dry your hands with paper towels.

poché aux œufs

escalfador de huevo

The poach is put on noodles.

porte pot

titular de la olla

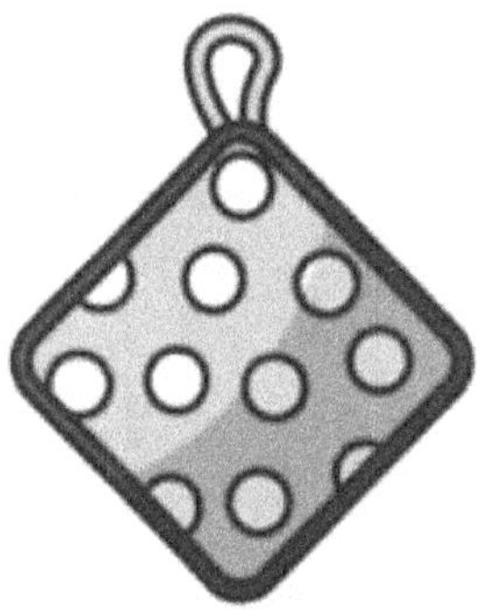

The potholder is soft.

rôti

asado

The chef made roast chicken.

rouleau à pâtisserie

rodillo

He is holding a rolling pin.

brouiller

lucha

My mom is making scrambled
eggs for breakfast.

mijoter

hervir a fuego lento

The simmer is rice today.

couteau

cuchillo

The knife is sharp.

cuillère

cuchara

I eat my food with a spoon and
fork.

spatule

espátula

The spatula will help us flip the steak over.

vapeur

vapor

The steam is coming from the pot.

passoire

colador

The strainer is used to strain stuff.

minuteur

temporizador

I set my timer for 12:00.

fourchette

tenedor

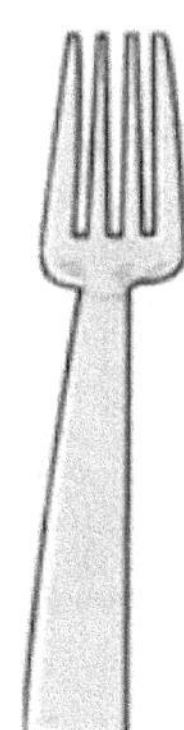

I have lots of metallic forks.

grille-pain

tostadora

The toaster will toast my bread.

bouilloire

tetera

The kettle has tea inside.

réfrigérateur

refrigerador

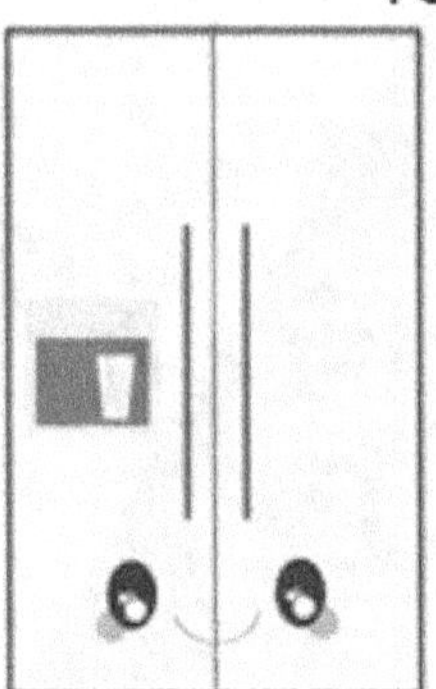

The refrigerator has lots of things inside.

mixeur

licuadora

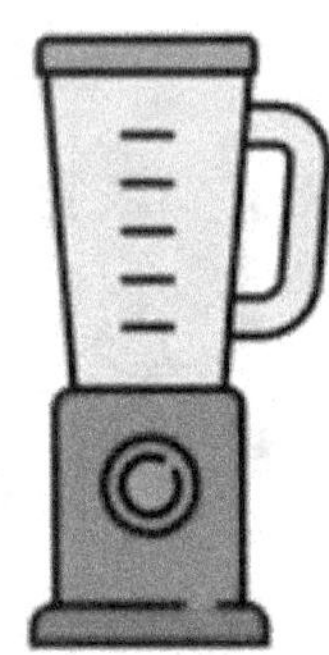

The blender will mix up my fruits.

cabinets

gabinetes

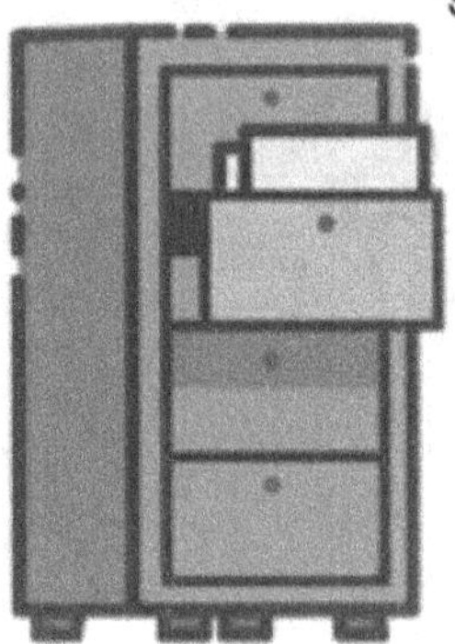

The cabinet has my paper inside.

placard

alacena

The cupboard has lots of books.

four micro onde

microonda

The microwave will heat my food.

arrière

espalda

She has a slender back.

des joues

las mejillas

She kisses her mom on the cheek.

poitrine

cofre

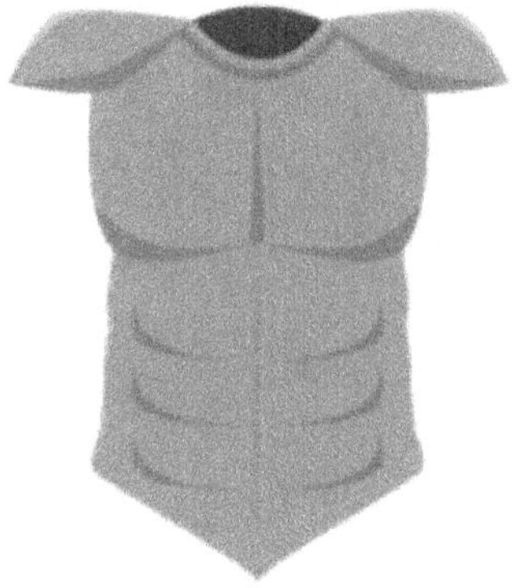

The armor is for your chest.

menton

barbilla

This is my chin!

oreilles

orejas

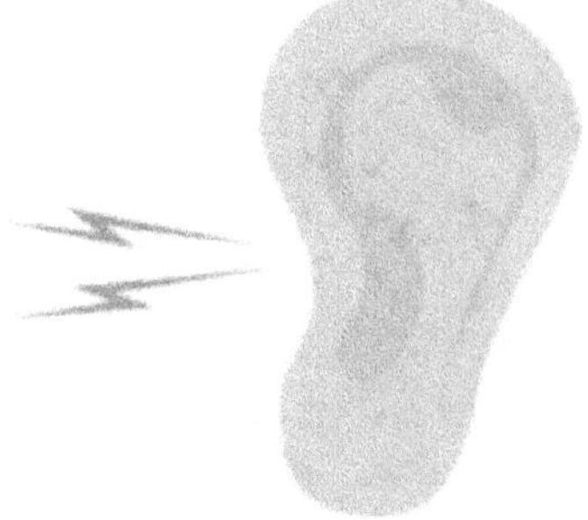

The ear is hearing something.

les sourcils

cejas

The eyebrows are raised.

yeux

ojos

The eyes are blue.

pieds

pies

I have one pair of feet.

des doigts

dedos

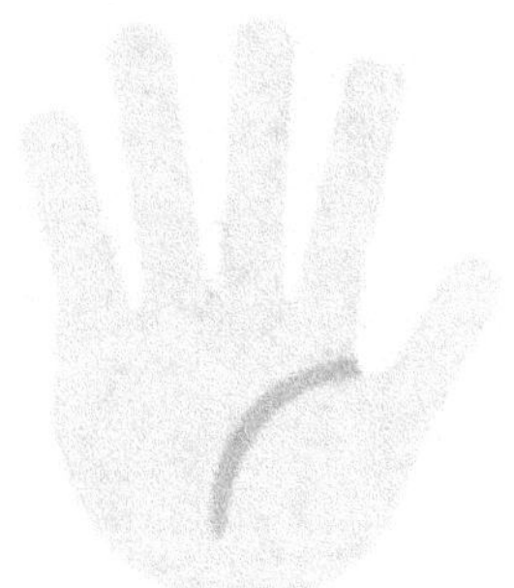

The fingers are waving at us.

pied

pie

My foot has five fingers.

front

frente

My brain is behind my forehead.

cheveux

cabello

My hair is long and black.

mains

manos

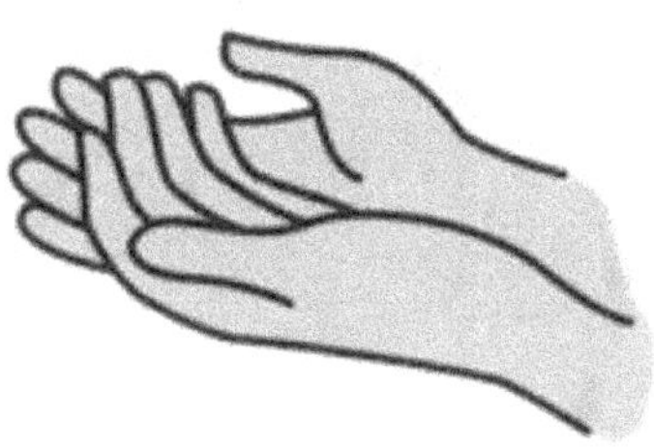

I will wash my hands in the sink.

tête

cabeza

She has a big head.

les hanches

caderas

The gorilla has his hands on his hips.

les genoux

rodillas

She is begging on her knees.

jambes

piernas

The tiger has strong legs.

lèvres

labios

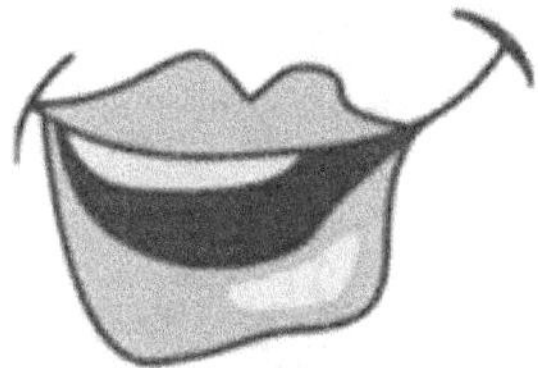

The lips have lipstick on.

bouche

boca

He is covering his mouth with his hand.

cou

cuello

The necklace is very special to me.

nez

nariz

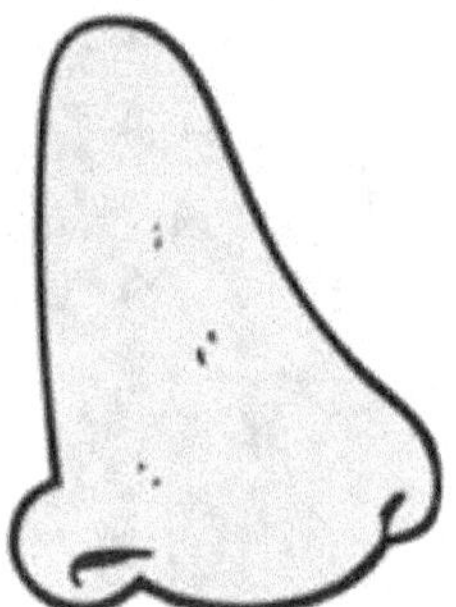

The nose smells something.

épaules

espalda

He puts his hands on his shoulders.

estomac

estómago

He has a big stomach.

les dents

dientes

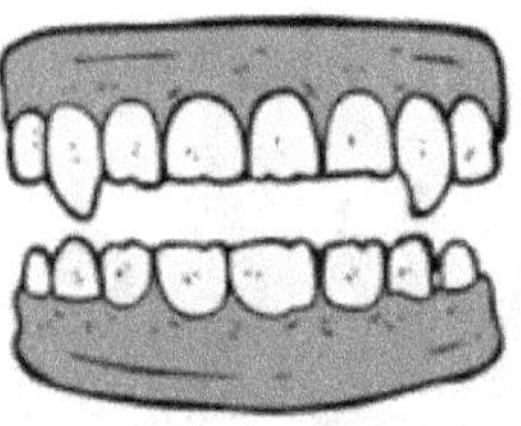

The teeth are clean and white.

gorge

garganta

He has a sore throat today.

les orteils

dedos de los pies

My toes are small.

langue

lengua

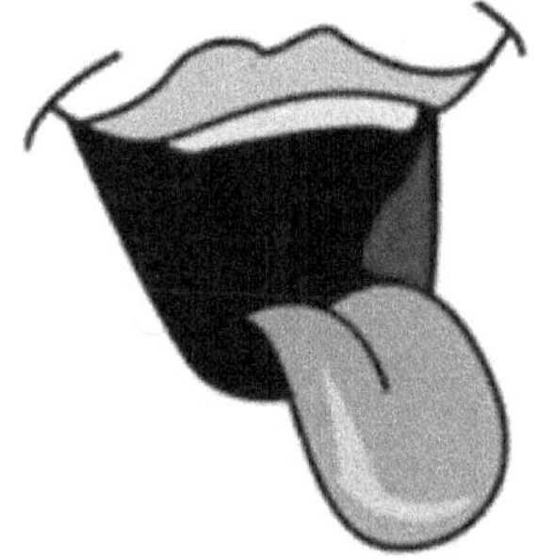

My tongue is licking ice cream.

dent

diente

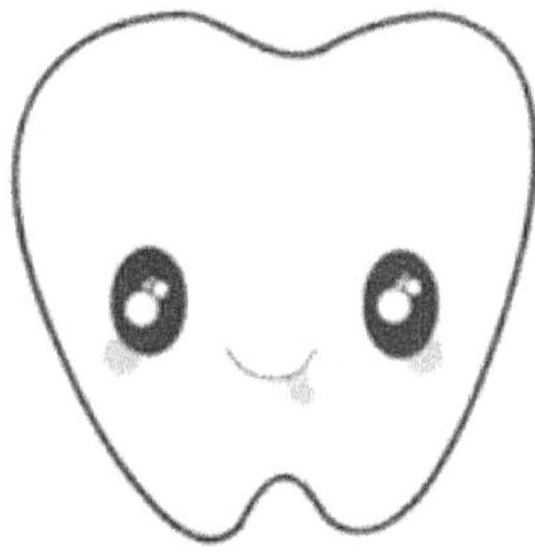

The tooth has big eyes.

taille

cintura

He has his hands on his waist.

salopette

mono

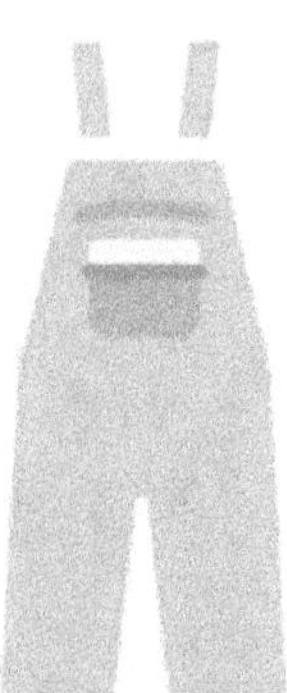

I bought these overalls for you!

mitaines

mitones

The mittens are very warm.

bonnet

gorro

The beanie is for winter.

tablier

delantal

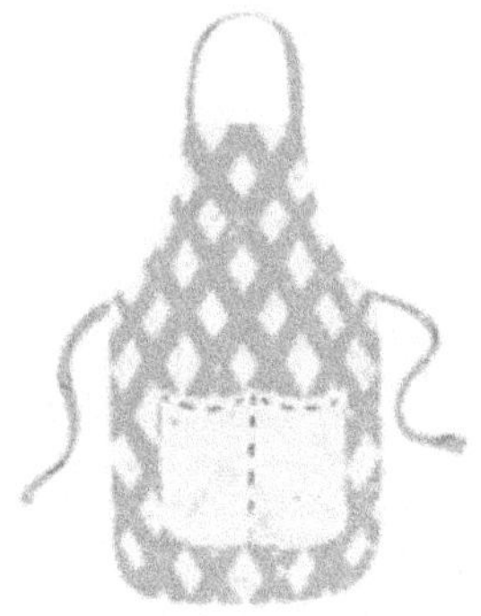

I wear my apron when I bake.

poupée

muñeca

The doll is for my baby sister.

hochets

sonajas

The rattle is for the baby.

jouet

juguete

The toy is very fun.

couche

pañal

The baby has to wear a diaper.

berceau

moisés

She is sleeping in her bassinet.

bavoir

babero

My baby brother has to wear his
bib when he is eating.

octogone

octágono

The octagon is saying okay!

triangle

triángulo

The triangle has three corners.

carré

cuadrado

Square

The square has four sides.

cercle

circulo

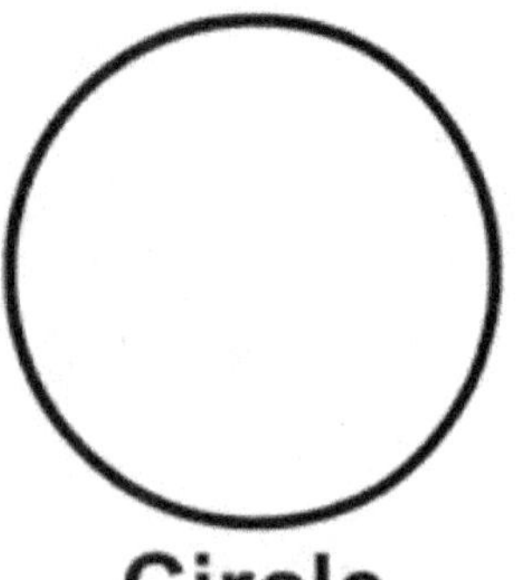

Circle

The circle is round.

ovale

oval

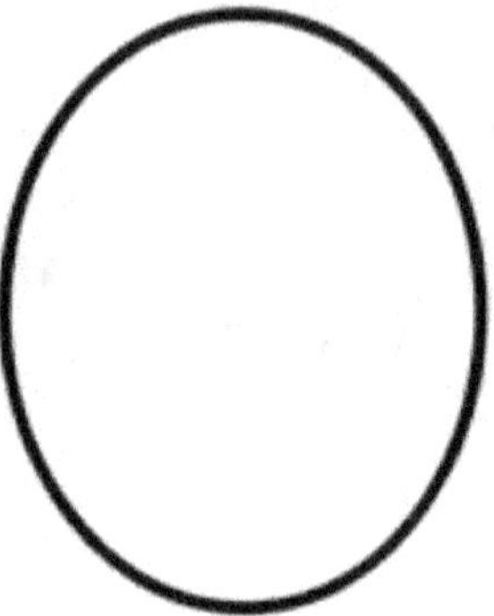

The oval shape looks like a circle.

cœur

corazón

I drew a heart on my paper.

traverser

cruzar

That sign is a cross.

la flèche

flecha

The arrow is pointing this way.

cube

cubo

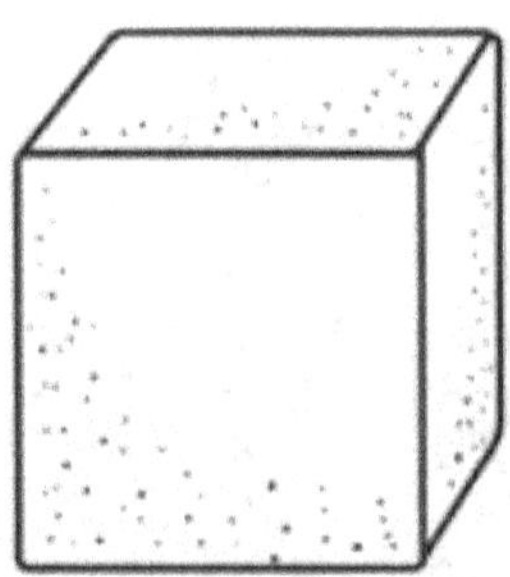

The cube is 3D.

étoile

estrella

The star is yellow and shiny.

tir à l'arc

tiro al arco

The archery is where you aim.

badminton

bádminton

My favorite sport is badminton.

criquet

grillo

I am very good at cricket.

bowling

bolos

I got one pin down at bowling!

boxe

boxeo

The boxing gloves are hot.

tennis

tenis

He can hit the ball in tennis.

faire de la planche a roulettes

skateboarding

He skateboards to school.

planche de surf

tabla de surf

The shark loves surfing in the ocean.

le hockey

hockey

I like to play Ice hockey.

yoga

yoga

He is closing his eyes and doing yoga.

épée

esgrima

They are fencing and dueling together.

aptitude

aptitud

She will do some fitness in the pool.

gymnastique

gimnasia

He can do brilliant gymnastics.

karaté

kárate

She is good at kicking in Karate.

volley-ball

vóleibol

She is holding a volleyball.

musculation

levantamiento de pesas

The girl with brown hair can do weightlifting.

basketball

baloncesto

He can balance the ball with one finger in basketball.

base-ball

béisbol

The little chick is in the finales at baseball.

le rugby

rugby

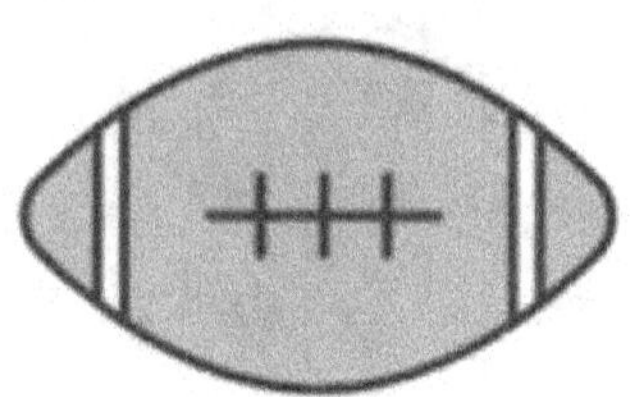

The rugby ball has white stripes.

lutte

lucha

The sumo will compete in wrestling.

course de voitures

carrera de coches

He is number one for car racing.

cyclisme

ciclismo

He is peacefully cycling on the road.

fonctionnement

corriendo

He is running while listening to his earphones.

tennis de table

tenis de mesa

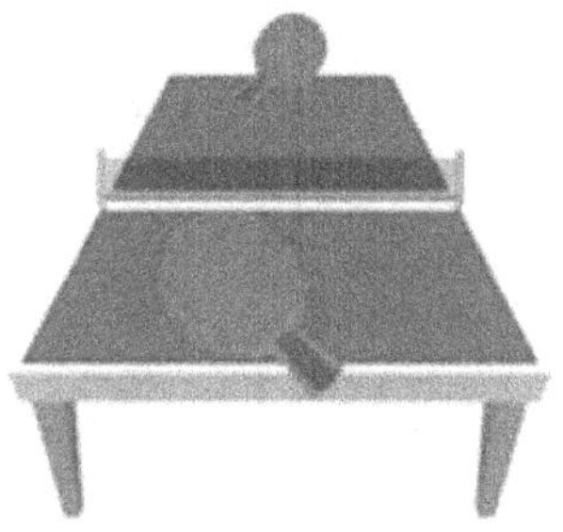

My brother and dad will play table tennis.

pêche

pescar

He will go to the river to fish.

judo

judo

She has a red belt in Judo.

escalade

alpinismo

He will climb the ladder.

tournage

disparo

He is shooting the archery board.

le golf

golf

She is going to compete in the golf competition.

balade

paseo

He will ride his scooter.

asseyez-vous

siéntate

They are sitting down together.

se lever

levántate

She likes to stand up.

bats toi

lucha

They are fighting over the book.

rire

risa

He is laughing so hard!

lis

leer

She read a picture book.

jouer

jugar

He went to play on the slide.

ecoutez

escucha

He listened for the ice cream cart.

pleurer

llorar

He cried because he got a bad grade.

pense

pensar

He thought that the test would be hard.

chanter

canta

He sang for the concert.

regarder la télévision

mirar televisión

He watched TV the whole night.

danse

baile

She was a good dancer.

allumer

encender

The light is turned on.

éteindre

apagar

The light is turned off.

gagner

ganar

He won the contest.

mouche

volar

The parrot can fly.

couper

cortar

He was cutting his nails.

désinvolte

tirar a la basura

He threw away the garbage.

dormir

dormir

He slept soundly.

fermer

cerca

He closed his mouth shut.

ouvert

abierto

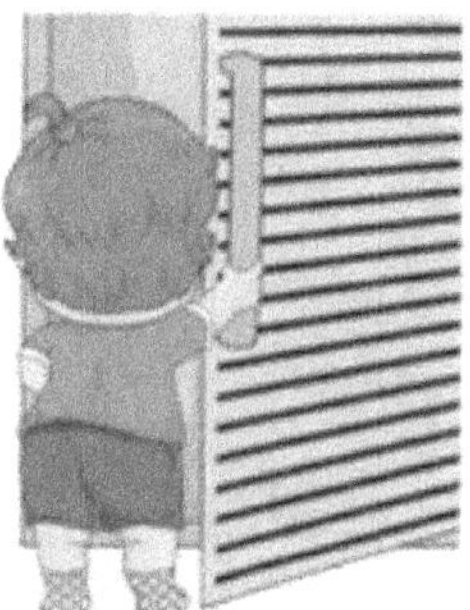

She opened the bathroom door.

écrire

escribir

She wrote with a pencil.

donner

dar

Santa gave her a present.

sauter

saltar

She had fun jumping.

manger

comer

The shark ate yummy ice cream.

boisson

beber

The old British man drank tea.

cuisinier

cocinar

The microwave cooked his soup.

lavage

lavar

You need to remember to wash your hands.

attendre

espere

He was waiting for the bus.

montée

subida

She climbed a lot of mountains.

parler

hablar

Two best friends were talking together.

crawl

gatear

The baby crawled on the floor.

rêver

sueño

The Sloth dreamed about eating leaves.

creuser

cavar

That strong man dug a swimming pool.

taper

aplaudir

The baby clapped her hands.

tricoter

tejer

She knits with the purple string.

coudre

coser

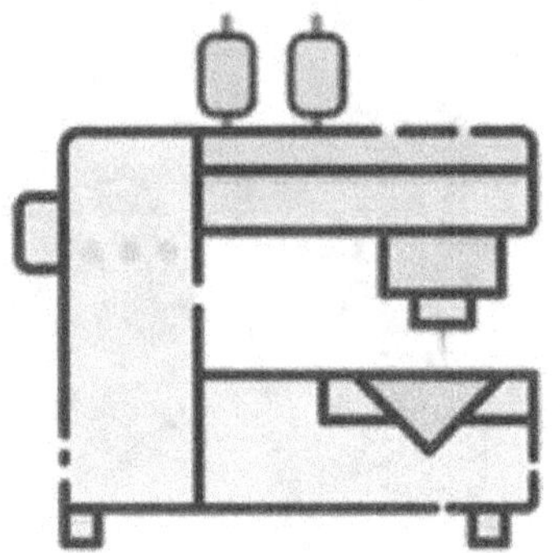

That is a sewing machine.

odeur

oler

The perfume smelled great.

baiser

beso

He kissed his mother.

étreinte

abrazo

They hugged each other.

ronfler

ronquido

The tiger snored.

baigner

bañarse

He took a bath.

s'incliner

reverencia

He bowed to the judge.

peindre

pintar

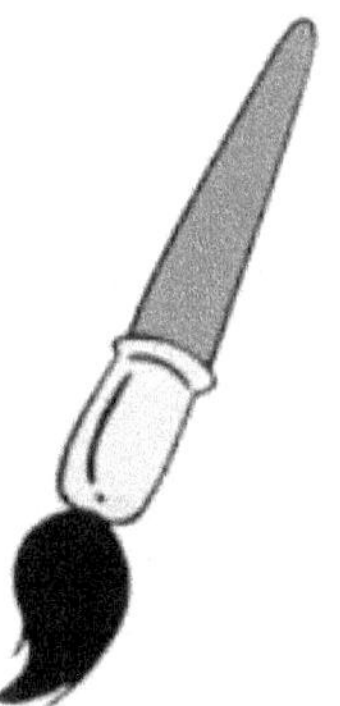

He painted a colorful picture.

se plonger

bucear

He dove to the deepest part of the ocean.

ski

esquí

The ski was expensive.

empiler

apilar

The books are stacked high.

acheter

comprar

They bought cereal.

secouer

sacudir

They shook hands together.

programmeur

programador

He was a smart computer programmer.

vétérinaire

veterinario

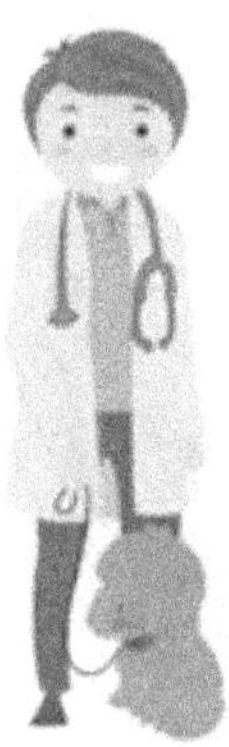

She is a veterinarian.

vendeur de rue

vendedor ambulante

That street vendor sells hot dogs.

mineur

minero

That Miner will find gold.

prof

profesor

The owl is the teacher.

groom

botones

That Bellboy is fat.

orateur

altavoz

The chicken is a great Speaker.

boucher

carnicero

The Butcher sells fish.

pharmacien

farmacéutico

That Pharmacist saved a person's life.

réceptionniste

recepcionista

He is a Receptionist.

politicien

político

He wants to be a Politician.

guide touristique

guía turístico

That Tour guide led us around Japan.

entrepreneur

empresario

He is an Entrepreneur.

danseuse de ballet

bailarina de ballet

She is training to be a Ballet dancer.

astronaute

astronauta

He is a great astronaut.

juge

juez

That Judge is always fair.

avocat

abogado

The lawyer is serious.

la caissière

cajero

She is a cashier at the market.

conducteur de taxi

conductor de taxi

He is a fast Taxi driver.

plombier

fontanero

That Plumber fixes toilets.

musicien

músico

She wants to be a Musician like her teacher.

chef

cocinero

The chef makes fast food.

boulanger

panadero

That baker is a bread.

artiste

artista

That Artist came from Italy.

acteur

actor

That actor is famous.

barman

tabernero

The Bartender works in a bar.

coiffeur

peluquero

That girl is a Hairdresser.

évêques

obispos

He is a Bishop.

opticien

óptico

She went to an Optician.

fleuriste

florista

She is a great Florist.

écrivain

escritor

He is a famous author.

comptable

contador

My accountant is loyal.

du vin

vino

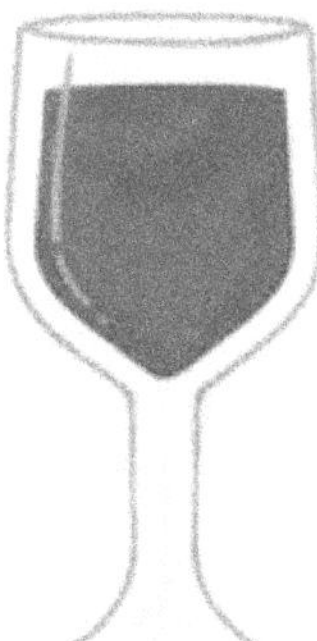

That wine tastes good.

café

café

That coffee is bitter.

limonade

limonada

The lemonade is refreshing.

chocolat chaud

chocolate caliente

I drink hot chocolate every day.

milk-shake

malteada

The milkshake has whipped cream.

eau

agua

The water is not cold.

thé

té

The tea is hot.

lait

leche

Milk is white.

bière

cerveza

The beer is foamy.

un soda

soda

The soda is fizzy.

smoothie

zalamero

The smoothie is a watermelon flavor.

milk-shake

malteada

The milkshake has whipped cream.

lait de coco

leche de coco

The coconut milk is yummy.

du jus d'orange

zumo de naranja

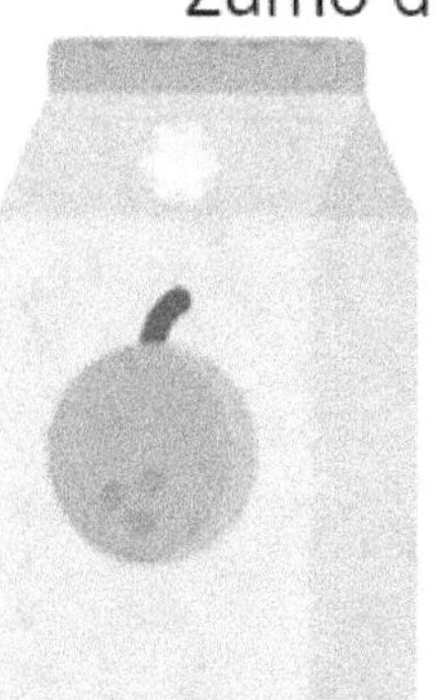

The orange juice is made from oranges.

cacao

cacao

The cocoa is sweet.

fromage

queso

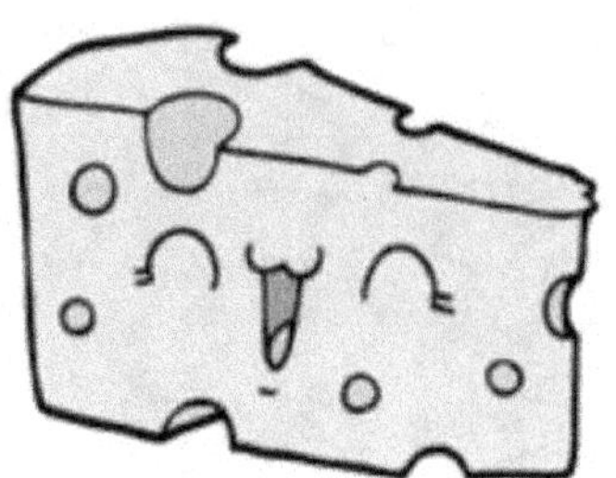

The cheese is creamy.

oeuf

huevo

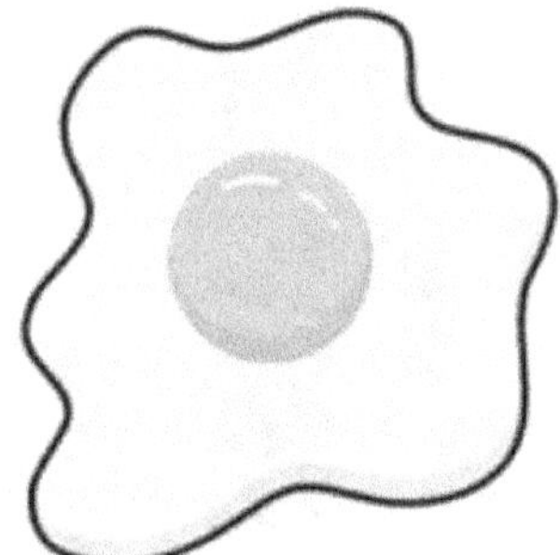

The egg is fried.

beurre

mantequilla

The butter is put on bread.

margarine

margarina

Margarine looks like butter.

yaourt

yogur

That yogurt is popular.

cottage cheese

queso cottage

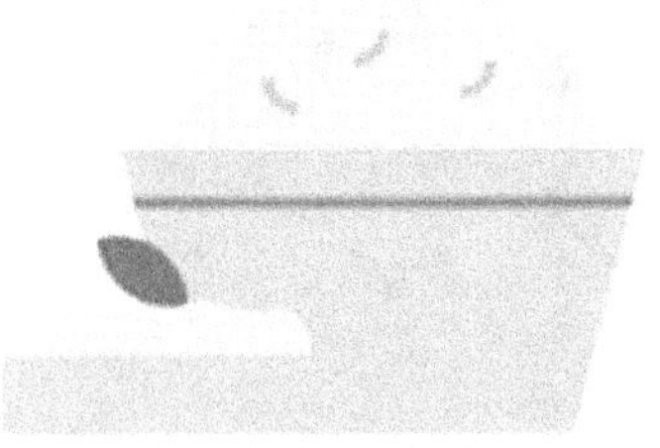

The cottage cheese is put on crackers.

crème glacée

helado

They have a triple scoop ice cream.

crème

crema

That is a lot of creams.

sandwich

emparedado

That sandwich is healthy.

saucisse

salchicha

Americans love sausages.

hamburger

hamburguesa

That hamburger looks happy.

hot-dog

pancho

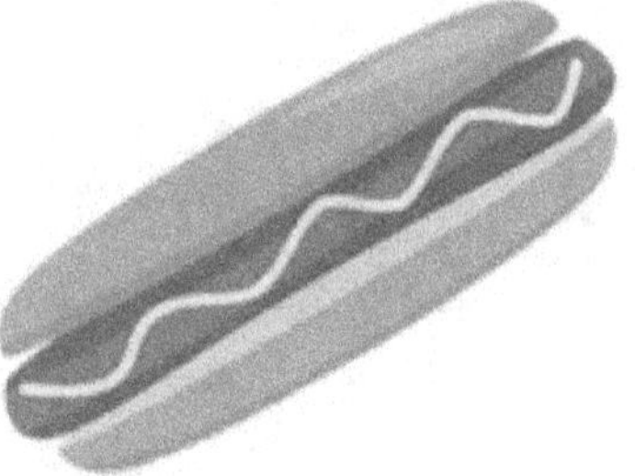

That hot dog has mustard on it.

pain

pan de molde

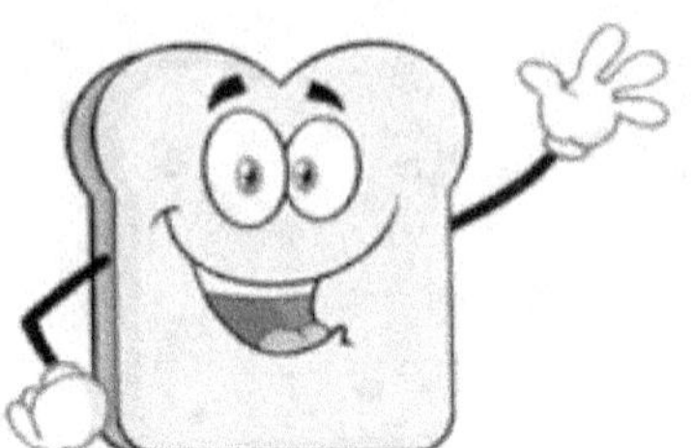

That bread is saying hello.

pizza

pizza

That pizza is cheesy.

steak

filete

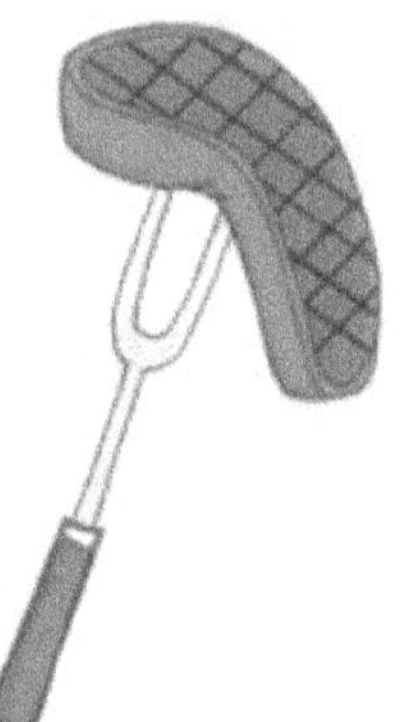

The steak was grilled.

poulet rôti

pollo asado

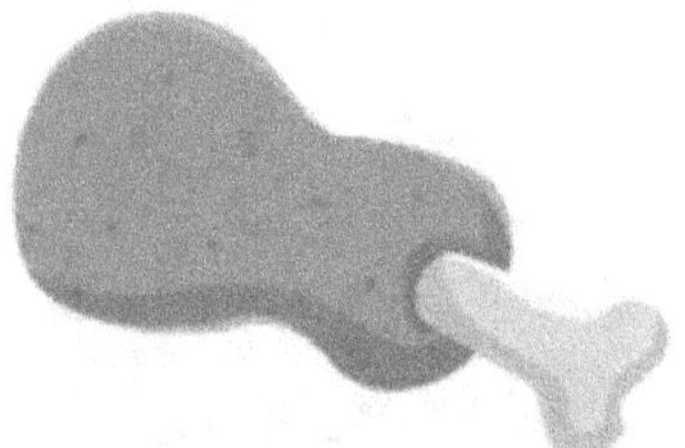

Roast Chicken is delicious.

poisson

pez

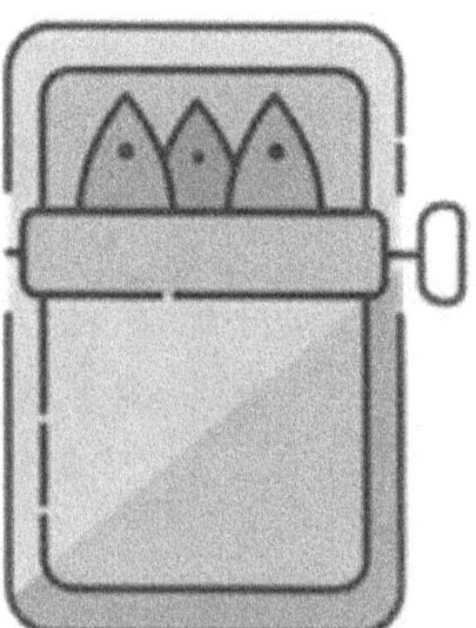

You can buy canned fish in the market.

fruit de mer

mariscos

Lobster is expensive seafood.

jambon

jamón

Ham can be put in sandwiches.

kebab

brocheta

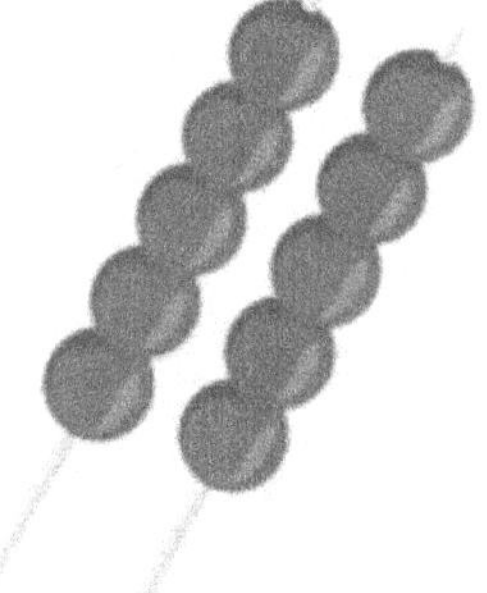

Kebab is a delicacy in America.

bacon

tocino

That bacon is smiling.

crème fraîche

crema agria

You can dip your chips in sour cream.

vache

vaca

Cows are black and white.

lapin

conejo

That rabbit is fun to play with.

canard

pato

That duck is content.

crevette

camarón

The shrimp has six legs.

porc

cerdo

That pig is pink and fat.

abeille

abeja

The bee has a stinger.

chèvre

cabra

That goat has a white horn.

crabe

cangrejo

The crab has two big pincers.

cerf

ciervo

That deer is sleeping.

dinde

pavo

The turkey has a giant tail.

colombe

paloma

That dove is carrying a plant.

mouton

oveja

That sheep has fluffy wool.

poisson

pez

That fish has colorful fins.

poulet

pollo

That chicken is waking everybody up.

cheval

caballo

The horse has a red mane.

chaise

silla

That wing chair is yellow.

meuble tv

soporte tv

The TV stand can hold books.

canapé

sofá

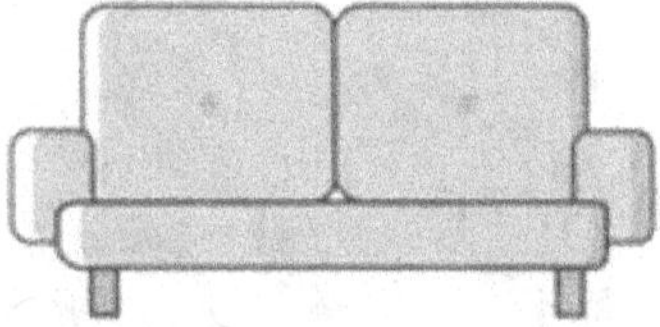

The sofa is comfortable to sit on.

coussins

cojines

The cushion helps soften your seat.

téléphone

teléfono

The telephone is ringing.

télévision

televisión

That television is big.

haut-parleurs

altavoces

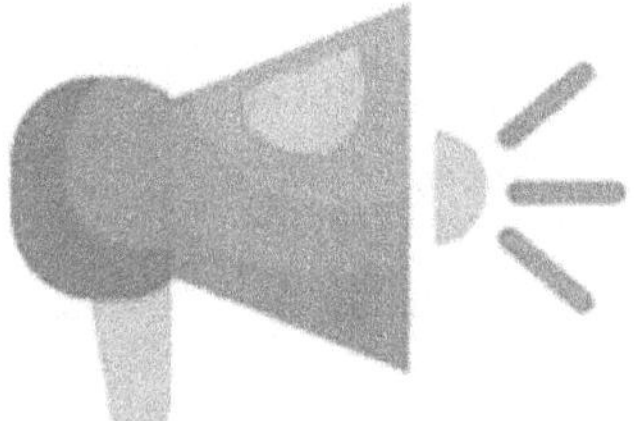

That speaker is used to increase the volume.

table d'appoint

mesa auxiliar

That end table is sparkling clean.

service à thé

juego de té

That tea set is from China.

cheminée

hogar

The fireplace makes me warm.

télécommandes

controles remotos

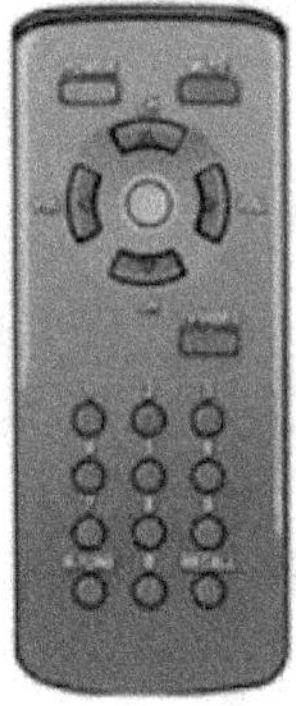

The remote has lots of buttons.

ventilateur électrique

ventilador eléctrico

The fan is blowing wind.

lampadaire

lámpara de piso

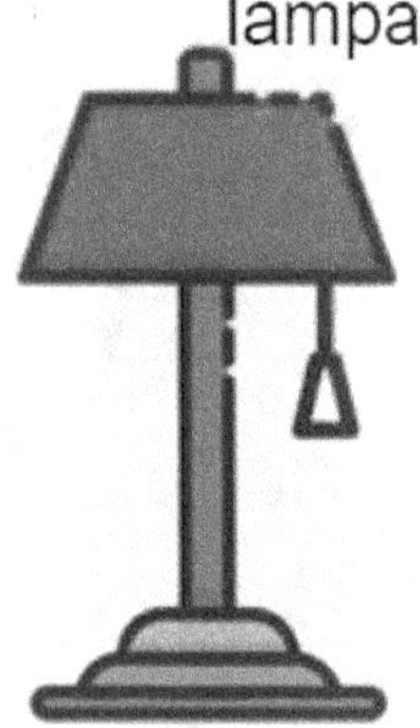

The floor lamp is very tall.

tapis

alfombra

The carpet is soft and silky.

bureaux

escritorios

The table is made of wood.

stores

persianas

I will pull the blinds down.

rideaux

cortinas

She opened the curtains.

image

imagen

The picture is about the mountains and the sky.

vase

florero

The roses are all in a vase.

l'horloge

reloj

The alarm clock is beeping.

oreiller

almohada

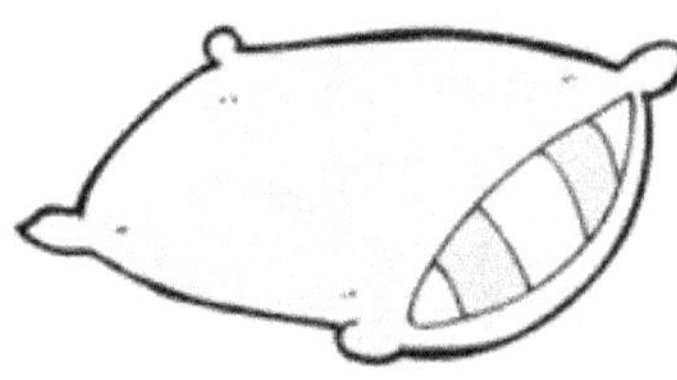

The pillow is pink and yellow.

cintre

percha

The hat stand has only one hat on it.

mettre la table	lampe de table

mettre la table

tocador

I have made up on my dressing table.

lampe de table

lámpara de mesa

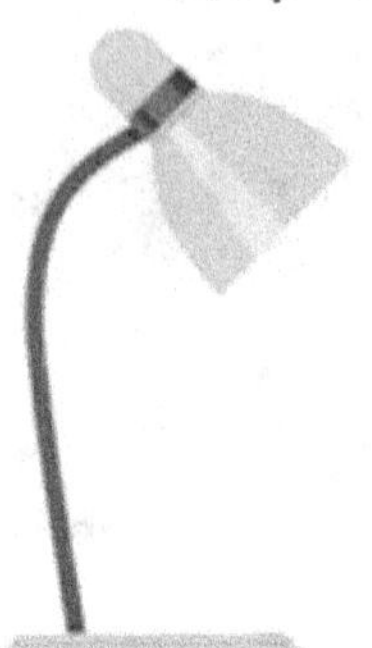

The table lamp will help me see in the dark.

miroir

espejo

The mirror is very tall.

planche a repasser

tabla de planchar

Don't touch the ironing board, it's hot!

boîte avec tiroir

caja con cajon

You can keep your clothes in the hope chest.

table de chevet

mesilla de noche

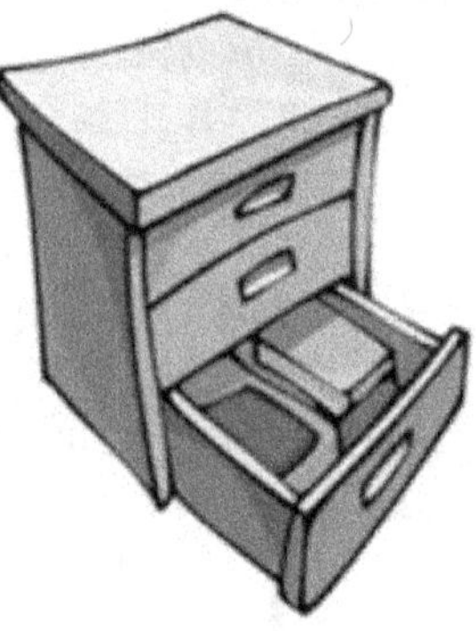

The nightstand has my lamp on it.

lit

cama

The bed is charming.

climatisation

aire acondicionado

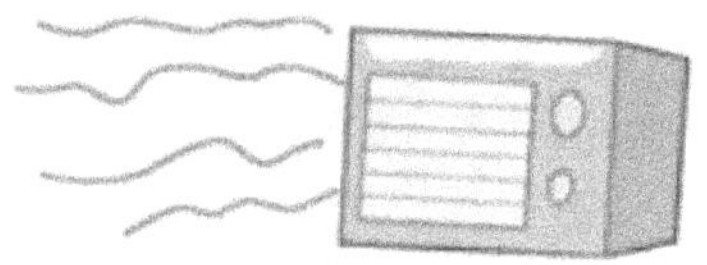

The air conditioner is cold.

cruche

jarra

The measuring jug has nothing inside.

dentifrice

pasta dental

The toothpaste is mint flavored.

brosse à dents

cepillo de dientes

The toothbrush has toothpaste on it.

savon

jabón

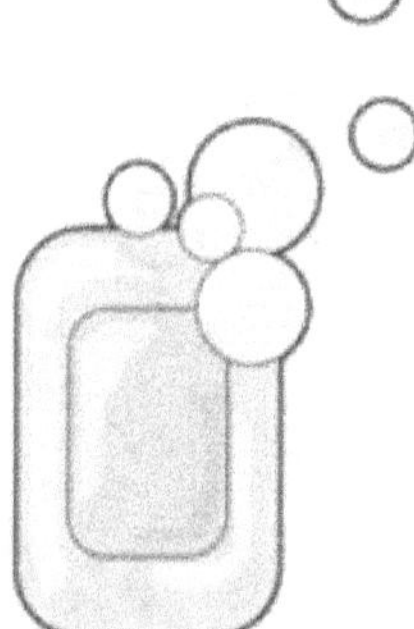

The soap is very bubbly.

pince à linge

pinza de ropa

The clothespin will clip my clothes.

cintre

percha

The hanger is hanging my boots.

sèche-cheveux

secador de pelo

The hairdryer will blow my hair.

shampooing

champú

The shampoo is used to clean your hair.

bulle

burbuja

The bubbles are very fun to play in.

brosse

cepillo

She is brushing her hair with the brush.

papier toilette

papel higiénico

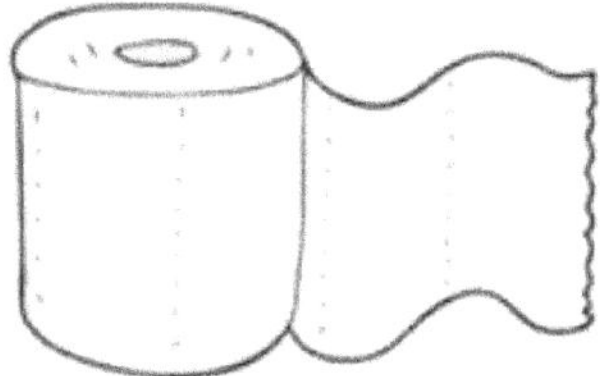

The toilet paper is used to dry your hands.

serviette

toalla

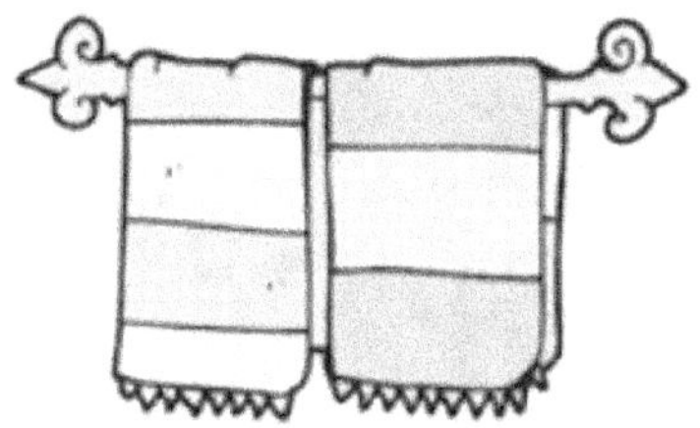

We have two towels on the rack.

corde à linge

tendedero

My shirt is hanging on the clothesline.

douche

ducha

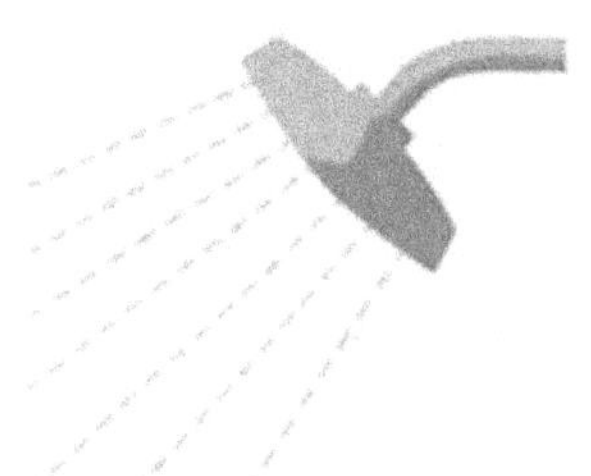

The shower is spraying water.

baignoire

bañera

The bathtub is comfortable.

lessive

detergente de lavandería

The laundry detergent is used with the washing machine.

seau

cubeta

Can you help me fill up the bucket?

vadrouilles

fregonas

The mop is used for mopping the floor.

savon liquide

jabón líquido

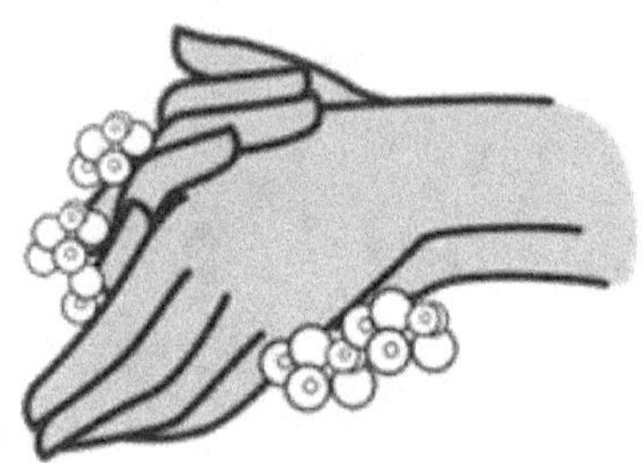

I use soapy water to wash my hands.

lessive en poudre

jabón en polvo

I will scoop up the washing powder.

sac poubelle

bolsa de basura

The trash bag is full of trash.

poubelle

bote de basura

You have only to put recylcle trash in the trash can.

les puits

fregaderos

You should wash your hands in the sink.

cuvette des toilettes

inodoro

She let her bunny use the toilet.

machine à laver

lavadora

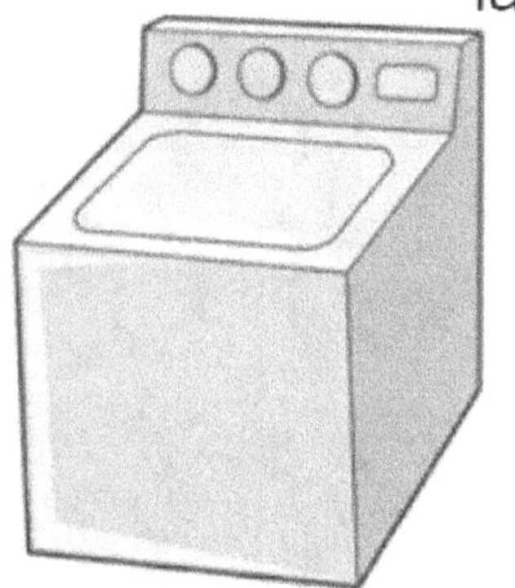

The washing machine wash your clothes.

panier à linge

cesto de la ropa

She is putting all the clothes into the laundry basket.

le rasoir

maquinilla de afeitar

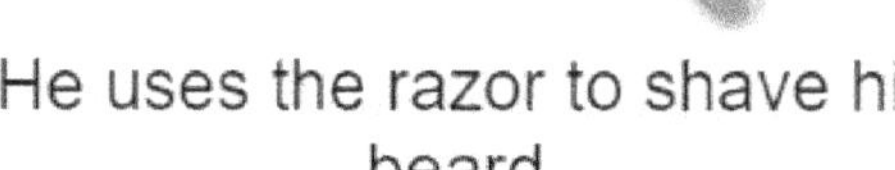

He uses the razor to shave his beard.

rasoir électrique

afeitadora eléctrica

The electric razor works faster than the normal one.

crème à raser

crema de afeitar

The shaving cream is fluffy.

bain de bouche

enjuague bucal

The mouthwash smells very lovely.

coton-tige

bastoncillo de algodón

Q-tip can be used for many things.

brosse à cheveux

cepillo de pelo

She brushes her hair with her hairbrush.

peigne

peine

Her dad will comb her hair for her.

nettoyant

limpiador

Put the cap back on the cleanser bottle.

échelle

escala

You can measure things on the scale.

papier de soie

pañuelo de papel

The tissue is on the counter.

jouets de bain

juguetes de baño

The little duck is a bath toy.

robinet

grifo

The faucet is broken.

miroir

espejo

He is looking in the mirror.

tapis de bain

alfombra de baño

The bath mat is purple and yellow.